1986

Contemporary
BICYCLE RACING

Contemporary

BICYCLE RACING

Keith Kingbay and George Fichter

cbi Contemporary Books, Inc.
Chicago

Library of Congress Cataloging in Publication Data

Kingbay, Keith.
    Contemporary bicycle racing.

    Includes index.
    1. Bicycle racing.   I. Fichter, George S.,
joint author.   II. Title.
GV1049.K56   1978   796.6   77-91158
ISBN 0-8092-7558-9
ISBN 0-8092-7654-2 pbk.

Published by Contemporary Books, Inc.
180 North Michigan Avenue, Chicago, Illinois 60601
Manufactured in the United States of America
Library of Congress Catalog Number: 77-91158
International Standard Book Number: 0-8092-7558-9 (cloth)
                                   0-8092-7654-2 (paper)

Published simultaneously in Canada by
Beaverbooks
953 Dillingham Road
Pickering, Ontario L1W 1Z7
Canada

Contents

Contemporary
BICYCLE RACING

A racer pours it on close to the finish, his muscles taut as he gives his machine every ounce of power possible. (Photo by William Dunlap.)

1

Most exciting, most demanding of all sports

Somebody once called it a "white noise." How else can a bicycle race be described? It defies a really rational, understandable description.

Compared to the roar of racing motor vehicles, the quiet is almost eerie. You hear only a whirr of wheels as the pack passes. At times even the crowd is silent, watching in a sort of hypnotic trance as the meld of muscles and machines moves almost fluidly around the track. Even a whisper can be heard from one side of the track to the other.

Breakaway

Then comes a breakaway. A racer pulls out of the pack and pours on power, his body and bicycle becoming a blur in his almost unbelievable surge of speed. The crowd is at first stunned by the sudden move. Then they begin to shout. Some cheer the daring of the racer who exploded from the pack and is now several lengths ahead. Others yell loudly to those behind to catch the speeding sprinter.

The calm has been transformed into a frenzy, and it sets the pack of racers afire, too. Conditioned leg muscles respond, and the bicycles shoot forward. The sprinter in front knew this would happen, of course, but he has done his computing. All he needs now is to hold his fractional lead for another hundred yards, and the race is won.

Bicycle racing is a tough sport. The racers need not only muscles but also wits, a perfect orchestration of brawn and brain. True, a few of the many kinds of races can be won by sheer strength or endurance, but most demand strategy as well. The racer must be as wily as a fox in deciding what moves to make, sometimes feinting to put his opponents off guard and then turning loose all of his power at a well-calculated moment to give him the winning advantage.

For most people in the United States, bicycle racing is a new sport. Until very recent times, it attracted almost no spectators and very few contestants, but in other parts of the world, especially Europe and Latin America, it is a major sport. In these places, bicycle racers are the highest paid of all athletes, and the champions are national heroes. This was true also in the United States until the 1930s. When bicycling became a mania in the 1890s, bicycle racing also emerged as a popular expression of bicycling proficiency. Many of the world champions in those days were Americans, and the six-day races that were organized in New York's Madison Square Garden go by the name of "Madisons" to this day.

Speed records

A look at the ultimate—the speed records achieved on bicycles—really tells the story. These are races of one man and his wheels against all the odds of competition, the weather, fate, and the clock. The first notable record was set by Charles "Mile-A-Minute" Murphy, an American. In 1899, he rode his bicycle behind a train at a measured 62.3 miles per hour in a record 574/5 seconds. For many years, this

In paced speed records, the racer rides behind a machine that breaks the wind. In effect, the racer rides in a vacuum to achieve the incredible speeds. Note the size of the front sprocket on bicycle.

record went unbroken. Slowly, however, the speed began to creep up, and in 1942, the mark of 100 miles per hour was passed by Alf Letourneur. He spun his wheels over the road at 108.9 miles per hour, a fantastic achievement. Then another Frenchman, Jose Meiffret, pushed the record up to 127.9 miles per hour. In 1973, the speed record came back to the United States when Dr. Al Abbott pedaled his bicycle across the Utah salt flats at the bulletlike speed of 138.6 miles per hour. And so the paced speed records have gone full circuit: from the Americans to the Europeans and then back again. Perhaps these feats of speed or endurance are symbolic, for in their stead is a revived wave of enthusiasm for racing in the United States. Once again Americans are showing increasing prowess in competitions both at home and abroad.

Gradual comeback

Unlike the meteoric return of recreational bicycle riding, the comeback of racing has been more gradual. To make it a success, attracting top athletes, the sport has needed both financial and spectator backing. Track racers, for example, must have velodromes, and these are now being built in a number of cities around the nation. Government officials have discovered that spending money for these facilities is politically acceptable—even wise. For similar reasons in the past, officials have been unwilling to sanction road races that required blocking off streets and highways while a race was being run. But they know now that a sufficiently large segment of the population wants these events. This includes not only the contestants and spectators but also the many businesses that profit when races are run in or through a community. Bicycle racing does indeed mean money for many segments of the population, and in this dimension it continues to grow.

For amateur athletes, bicycle racing represents the potential of a different kind of gold—the Olympic medals. Europeans have dominated the Olympics picture for many years—well over half a century, in fact. All this time, the Americans have in no way been a threat in the bicycling events. But that picture has changed, too. It began with places to train and with enthusiastic backing. American bicyclists are again pedaling toward the treasured Olympic gold with a dedication and determination that assures winners.

Racers in their saddles and ready to be pushed off in a mass-start race.
(Photo by Schwinn Bicycle Company.)

2

Racing bicycles and gear

Any bicycle that can be pedaled can also be raced, but if you want to compete in officially sanctioned bicycle races, you will ride a special machine. Racing bicycles are distinct from those ridden strictly for touring or for recreation. If you intend to do both road and track racing, then you will need one bicycle for each. There are also minor differences in bicycles used specifically for sprints and those used for pursuits or for other specialties.

Road races

Some touring bicycles are ridden in road races. For serious racing, however, the bicycle is lightweight—less than 25 pounds and averaging about 22. It is equipped with hand or caliper brakes and usually has a derailleur with 10 speeds (some to as many as 15) in which the gear ratios are much closer than in a regular touring bicycle. A bicycle racer is much more sensitive to slight changes in the demands on his

7

A road racer is much like a regular touring bicycle but is stripped of all excess weight items.

energy, and he uses his gears to maintain a steady pedaling tempo.

For racing, a bicycle is stripped to its absolute essentials to reduce its weight. It lacks carriers, fenders and other items that add weight but do not help the racer. Some racers become so obsessed with weight reduction that they bore holes in the components and further file their frames to cut down on the ounces they must move with their muscles. They engineer, or believe they do, the placement of the holes with care so that the strength of the component is not greatly affected. In all but the shortest races, a road rider equips his bicycle with a pump and a water bottle.

While the road-racing bicycle must be lightweight, it must also be strong. Generally, it is made of double-butted tubing—thicker at the ends than in the middle. Compared to that of the regular touring bicycle, a road-racing bicycle's frame has a steeper angle, though not as steep as a track racer's. It is therefore a bit more responsive than the touring bicycle but less so than the track bicycle. For road racing, a bicyclist rides lower (closer to the ground) than does a track racer.

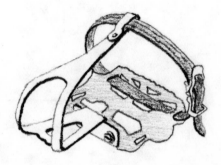

Toe clips and rat-trap pedals make it possible for bicyclist to give his machine full power in pedaling and to use "ankling" pedal technique.

Tires

Racing bicycles are equipped with a different type of tire known as a tubular. Tubular tires are made in many styles, and the type selected depends on the kind of race and the surface conditions. Basically, they are more responsive and lighter. Tire pressures are much higher than in ordinary tires. Pressures as high as 150 pounds per square inch are used in tires that weigh as little as 3½ ounces. The rims, too, are of a lighter construction. The tires are held to the rims by a mastic or shellac.

This lessened weight and added responsiveness means less energy is required to propel the machine. The light tires, with small road contact, make maneuvering easier, too. On long races, a spare (sometimes two) is carried along, tucked into the rear pocket of the jersey or under the saddle.

The bicycle has quick-release hubs for fast changing of the tires, rims, or wheels. The pedals have toe clips, assuring the bicyclist of being able to give full power to his pedaling.

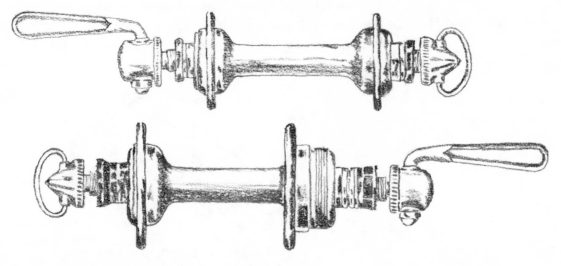

With quick-release hub mechanism, changing tires, rims, or wheels is possible with great speed. (Figure shows front hub above, rear hub below.)

Food and drink

In races longer than 25 miles, the rider's liquids are replaced by team members or friends from the side of the road. In many events, food is also handed up at specified feeding stations in musette bags. Many spectators feel that these feeding spots are the most fascinating parts of the race. They delight in watching the riders shift the food from the bags to the pockets of their jerseys and dispose of the empty bags and bottles. On many long races, a repair van follows with spare wheels and equipment, and in the staged or international events, each team is followed by a team car with spare bicycles as well as parts.

Custom-built bicycles

For cyclocross races, which are rough-and-tumble, cross-country events, a strengthened, customized road-racing bicycle is used, generally equipped with stronger wheels

Cyclo-cross racers ride strengthened road-racing bicycles that often must be carried long distances over rough terrain.

(often 40 spokes rather than the usual 36) and with heavier tires and rims. This is necessary because of the rough terrain. Some also have a special carrying handle to make it easier for the racer to pick up his machine for climbing clifflike slopes or for crossing fences or streams.

Some road-racing bicycles are custom built, but most are selected from stock bicycles and then modified to suit the racer's particular needs. Because they are made of the best materials and parts, a road-racing bicycle is also expensive, some costing more than a thousand dollars.

All track-racing bicycles are either custom built or are at least customized. If you are just beginning at racing, do not be hasty in having a bicycle specially made. Wait until

Track bicycles are stripped to the bare essentials, consisting only of a frame, pedals, handlebars, saddle, wheels, rims, and tires. There are no brakes, and the gears are fixed.

you are absolutely certain of your needs and the particular kind of racing on which you expect to concentrate. In terms of basic elements, a track bicycle is simple, consisting of a frame, pedals and handlebars, a saddle, and a set of wheels, rims, and tires. Compared to the fully equipped road machine, a track bicycle is much less expensive. The gear is fixed, so there is no shifting mechanism. The track bicycle also has no brakes. It is stopped by back pedaling while the racer at the same time puts a gloved hand on the front tire. The angle of the frame is usually steep, making the bicycle more responsive—a necessity in the close riding on tracks. The bottom bracket is high so that the bicycle can be laid over in banks without striking the pedals. Gear ratios on track bicycles can be changed quite easily to allow for varying conditions. In some events, especially in the younger age groups, gear ratios may be specified.

Track wheels, depending on the event, the track, and the rider, may have fewer spokes—to as few as 20. This makes them lighter but, of course, more subject to troubles. Track bicycles may be lighter in weight than road bicycles, but this depends, too, on their purpose.

Equipment

Like swimmers, bicycle racers often shave their legs to get rid of the hair. Partly this is to reduce whatever friction the hair might contribute to the bicyclist's movement through the air. It is also a safeguard to reduce the possibility of infection when there are cuts or "burns" from the spills on the road or the track and to facilitate rubdowns.

To protect his head, the racer wears a specially designed helmet that consists of one or two padded rims or bands that circle his head and two or more similar bands that run across the top of his head. The helmet is held in place with chin straps. In officially sanctioned events, all racers must wear approved helmets.

A bicycle racer's specially designed helmet gives full head protection, but is cool.

Jerseys worn by racers fit tightly—another design to reduce the friction and to make sure there is no drag due to a billowing of the garments. International rules specify that they must have short sleeves. Those worn in track races are usually tucked inside the racer's shorts. Those worn in road races are worn outside the shorts. Road jerseys have large pockets both in front and in back. These are filled with snack food or other items that the racer expects to use as he rides. Jerseys are usually brightly colored, the different bands of

A racing jersey is colorful, fits tightly, and has short sleeves.

Shorts are seamless, and
most have built-in chamois
seat and crotch, and have one
rear pocket.

color circling the garment horizontally or vertically. In
international events, the racers wear jerseys that display the
colors of their country. Jerseys are typically made of wool, a
combination of wool and cotton, or an acrylic to make them
fit tightly. Most riders prefer natural fibers for their absor-
bency. Track jerseys are often made of silk. In many long
road events, special jerseys are used to help the spectators
identify their heroes. The most famous of these is the yellow
jersey that signifies the leader in the Tour de France. Ameri-

Gloves have padded palms,
no fingers, and perforated
backs.

can champions are crowned by receiving the stars–and–stripes jersey. Only champions can wear this jersey in any sanctioned event.

Shorts are made either of wool or helenca, absorptive materials that "breathe." The shorts are equipped with soft, absorbent chamois pads appropriately placed for comfort. Racers typically do not wear undershorts because the seams are binding or abrasive on long rides. The color of regulation bicycle racing shorts is black, and the shorts are quite long. Although the rule is often not followed, they should reach within 5 inches of the knee.

Gloves worn by bicycle racers (and also many touring

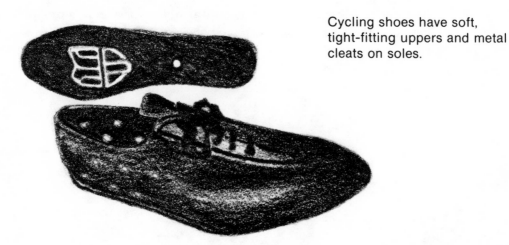

Cycling shoes have soft, tight-fitting uppers and metal cleats on soles.

bicyclists) do not have fingers. The palms are padded and the backs are perforated to let in air and to prevent a buildup of perspiration. The gloves protect the ulnar nerve from constant jarring in road races, and they are also used to whisk away any debris that has been picked up by the tires. In track races, the gloves are used to help "brake" the vehicle.

Bicycle racers wear special tight-fitting shoes. They have soft uppers but firm soles to which cleats are attached to fit into the slots of the toothed rat-trap pedals. When his feet are in place and the straps of the toe clips are drawn tight, the bicycle racer and his machine become literally a single unit.

Many road races include steep climbs. Racers usually ride in a pack until close to the finish. (Photo by John Libera.)

3

Road races

Bicycle racing got its start on the roads, then moved to the tracks. The beginning was probably prosaic, two or more proud and vigorous cyclists pitting their speed and endurance against each other in some unscheduled, unheralded impromptu event. From escapades of this sort came local champions and more formalized challenges, the duel of wheel against wheel taking on even greater proportions. Step by step, racing became organized: town champions against the champions of a neighboring town, then region against region, and finally national and world champions emerging, as rules and regulations governing the sport were also formed.

In the United States, road racing was very popular in the early days, but both interest and participation mysteriously waned in the 1930s. Now there is a revival, an increasing number of events being scheduled regularly throughout the country. Road races have one big disadvantage for spectators: in most events the racers are seen in action for only a limited portion of the race. Where suffi-

19

Most famous criterium race in the United States is New Jersey's Tour of Somerville. Note the crowd of spectators lining the street. (Photo by Schwinn Bicycle Company.)

cient enthusiasm has been generated either for particular racers or for special aspects of the race, however, a road race can be spectacular. The grueling Tour de France is probably the best-known single sporting event in the world, attracting participants from many countries and also the thousands of spectators who live on the streets and roads along most of the nearly 3,000 miles of the course. Millions watch the race on television.

Described here are the basic kinds of road races for which official records are kept. In almost every race, however, other kinds or variations may be used, and if they prove to be popular and worthwhile contests, they may become regular events. In recent years, for example, races with

large, multi-geared tricycles have grown in number, popularity, and sophistication, especially in street races. You may also see races on tandems, high-wheeled bicycles, or other kinds of pedaled vehicles. Whenever the owners of two vehicles of the same kind meet, the chances of a race are great.

Criterium races

These races are not only the shortest of the road races, but also offer spectators the best opportunity to see most of the event. Typically, the course is laid out on a blocked-off street in a town, and it may be as short as a mile or even less.

For the different classes of races, a varied number of laps is run, the total sometimes 50 miles or more. The shape of the course is determined by the streets. Usually, it is rectangular. If the course is laid out through a park or a similar kind of track, the curves, rises, and slopes may be gentle, but in a typical street situation, the turns are right angles. Steep hills to climb or to go down may also be part of the layout.

Primes or prizes are generally awarded at various stages of the race. Most of these are announced at the beginning, but some are spontaneous offerings from spectators who put up money or some prize to stimulate immediate action when they think the race is going too slowly. In many cases, a prime is given on each lap, so the racers are constantly pushing themselves at top speed to get as many as possible of the primes. Some racers enter the event only for the lap prizes and have no intention of completing the entire race. A bell or a horn is the signal that a prime is being offered for the coming lap. At the sprint finish, a number of racers may be moving close together in a tight pack. At this stage, the race becomes wildly furious, precisely the kind of action that spectators expect to see at a race.

Criterium races are often the first exposure people have to bicycle races. The sight of the racers in their colorful jerseys and their unbelievable performances do a good job of selling bicycle racing.

Speeds in criteriums differ according to the course and conditions, but 22 to 25 miles (35 to 40 kilometers) per hour is average.

Road time trials

Pitting bicyclists against the clock is a test of sheer speed rather than tactics or techniques. In the usual time-trial event, the racers are started at equal time intervals—usually one every minute. Passing is permitted, but racers may not pass closer than within 10 feet of the overtaken rider. Some racers strap stopwatches to their handlebars so they can watch their own time as they go. Distances vary, but the 25-mile (40-kilometer) time trial is most popular. Racers cover this distance in less than an hour. The course may be a straight line to some elected finish, although usually the ride may be to a designated turn and then back again.

Time trials with teams are also official events in the championship races. Each team typically consists of four men, started a minute apart. They ride in a line, and each man takes his turn at leading. The number of switches is determined by the length of the race. Time is marked for each team when its third man's front wheel crosses the finish.

On long-distance events, road racers are followed by a van with mechanics and coaches who keep bicycles in operating order and supply racers with food, drink and encouragement. (Photo by Keith Kingbay.)

Racer is passed a fresh bottle of water while he continues at full speed.
(Photo by John Libera.)

The long distance road race

Covering 50 miles (80 kilometers) or more, rarely less, the long distance race may be a circuit, from one town to another, or from the starting point out to a particular place and then back again. The course laid out commonly includes one or more hills to challenge the racers.

Road races are difficult to hold in many areas because government officials are reluctant to stop, reroute, or control automobile traffic during the race. Appreciation of road races is growing again, however. In some major events in Europe, for example, towns make special bids to have the course routed through their village because of the business generated by the race.

Stage races

These complex road races may last for several days or even weeks. The famous Tour de France, for example, is a stage race. It covers almost 3,000 miles and lasts for an average of 27 days. Built into the total event are time trials, criteriums, and other events that give each racer an opportunity to demonstrate his particular skills, and the winners of these events are given special time allowances. It is possible, however, for a racer to win the overall race by having the least total or accumulated time and yet not have been the winner of any single event along the way.

In stage races, each racer is followed by an entourage— a motorized vehicle in which his support team rides. These are the coaches, mechanics and others who keep him fed and give him water, advise him and suggest tactics. They also encourage the racer to do his best. They are his confidence during a hard day when he wonders whether going ahead is worth it.

Cyclocross races

These races are cross-country events in which much of the race is over such difficult terrain that the bicyclist must go on foot and carry his bicycle. The usual course covers three or four miles, sometimes with six or eight laps over the same circuit. Because some of the riding may be over grass or through sand, mud, loose soil or water, cyclocross racers use special tires to give them more traction and to reduce the blowout hazard. Racers who are serious about cyclocross races—and there are national and world championships both amateur and professional to be contested—spend a great amount of time practicing by riding over rough terrain, going up or down steps either on their bicycles or carrying them, and even perfecting their technique and speed of getting on and off their bicycles. Special pedals and shoes with running spikes are often used. In an actual race, a cyclocross racer pushes his vehicle to get up sufficient speed and then jumps into the saddle and slips his feet into his toe clips all in one swift movement.

Good hill climbers may try to steal the lead on a long, steep gradient—and then work hard to keep their position on the level. (Photo by John Libera.)

4

Riding to win in road races

Someone has said about bicycle races that you ride until you see black spots in front of your eyes, and then you keep on pedaling until they go away. It is best, of course, if you never see those black spots. They are actually a signal that you are running out of energy. They indicate that your fuel tank is empty. When they go away, your body has shifted to its reserves, like turning to the auxiliary tank in an automobile.

Eating and drinking

If you have been eating properly and are in prime condition, you should never get that feeling in a short race. But, in a long race, you will need refueling every two or three hours unless you have conditioned your body to perform long stints without more fuel intake. Some can do it without difficulty; others cannot. No other sport, with the possible exception of cross-country skiing, is so demanding.

Racer's food is put in a musette bag with a long shoulder strap. Racer puts arm through strap as he rides by. (Photo by Keith Kingbay.)

Because of the length of the events, road racers equip themselves with both food and drink. They fill their bottles with water, tea, or sometimes a juice, and if they have the bottle cage mounted on the handlebar stem, they may drink with a straw as they continue to go full tilt. When one bottle is emptied, a fresh one is passed to them by their coach or a member of their racing team. Sometimes the bottle is handed up to them while they continue at full speed. This is a bit risky, however, and the misses can be hazardous to other racers. Missed and discarded bottles must also be retrieved, requiring that someone go onto the course. The safest way is for a trainer to run alongside the racer holding the bottle by its neck so the racer can grab it firmly as he whisks by.

Food can also be passed to a racer by teammates or trainers. Someone stands at the side of the road holding a musette bag filled with kinds of food that will replenish the exhausted rider's energy and that can be eaten while he stays in the saddle. The bags have long shoulder straps, and the racer simply sticks an arm through the loop as he goes by.

The rear pockets of racing jerseys were put there specifically for carrying food, and in times gone by, there were also large pockets in front. Depending on the length of the ride or course, most racers stuff these pockets with food before they set out. Each racer may carry a different kind of food. This is due not only to personal preferences but also to his conviction that particular kinds are more satisfying and provide more energy. For some, oranges are perfect thirst quenchers while at the same time they do give some energy. Others carry bags containing a mixture of nuts and raisins or other dried fruits. Some like bananas; others want peanut butter and jelly sandwiches. When a racer becomes really hungry and is about ready to bonk out, he is not fussy about what he puts into his stomach. If it will give him energy quickly, it's perfect.

Tactics

Road races—and particularly the long-distance events—call for a great deal of maneuvering and tactics. Your training rides should prepare you for most of the circumstances that will be encountered. For criteriums, you should, for example, practice taking turns at high speed, and you should be able to shift gears, if necessary, so that you keep the same pedaling rhythm. The constant deceleration and acceleration are especially debilitating. In preparing for road events, do some hill climbing and learn how to judge accurately when you can roll over the top without needing to change gears or when a shift is necessary without danger of losing speed or tempo. On very steep hills, of course, a lower gear is demanded, and it may be necessary to stand on the pedals to give your machine sufficient power. Pushing forward with your body at the same time helps, aiding the pedaling with arms and shoulders. Avoid the wasteful wobbling from side to side.

You can do all of your training rides alone, but it is highly important that you learn to be comfortable when you ride in groups. Do not turn your training rides into races, of course. Save your energy and top speeds for actual racing events. But sprints now and then to test yourself against a competitor can bolster your confidence and prime you for the real encounters.

By the time you are entering actual races, you should know fairly well how you measure against other racers, but it will take a number of races to give you the experience needed to make the best decisions. You may, for example, realize that you can never match the bursts of speed of some sprinters at the finish, but that you have more stamina for long distances. You can win only by building up to a high, sustained speed early in the race and then holding it. To keep up with you, the sprinters will risk tiring themselves too early in the event. Don't attack each time someone goes past you. Recognize the threats. Learn to work with several others. Lone attacks early in an event are rarely successful. If your plans are successful, the sprinters will have lost the urge to sprint long before the finish. On the other hand, if you are a good sprinter, you may decide that it is wisest to stay somewhere near the middle of the pack, drafting and saving every ounce of energy for the finish. Learn to follow a wheel closely and to recognize the riders who will be close to the lead at the finish. Then you can unleash all of your reserves to explode around the others and over the finish line.

In every instance possible, go over the course at least once before the race. This gives you an opportunity to know ahead of time where there are straightaways, where there are hills, gradients, and curves, and other special features. It eliminates the surprises that could be costly if you are not prepared for them. Also, study the racing program. If you have raced before, you will see many familiar names and will know what to expect of them. Memorize their numbers and jerseys so that you can identify them at a glance when you are racing. Watch the performances of the newcomers. See if they show promise of being threats in future events.

As you progress, you may decide to try taking it from the front. It's almost impossible to do this alone. Prearrange with several others to steal away after a particular sprint, a climb, or some other preselected spot. A small, well-matched group is extremely difficult to catch.

Practice staying close to some of the good riders. Learn their strong points and their failings. Learn your own and how to outwit the other guy. That's the name of the game.

Stay close to the front in a large pack, especially on a course with turns and hills. The back part of the pack is erratic, going first slow and then fast as the racers continuously chase each other and wear themselves out. All of this is easily said on paper, of course, but doing it takes practice.

You and your friends may decide to make your move just after there has been a furious sprint for a prime. Those who have poured it on for the prime will almost automatically slacken a bit after going over the finish. By the time they realize what has happened, you will be too far ahead to be caught. They may think you will get tired and that they can overtake you later, but don't let them. Once you get a gap between you and the pack, keep it.

Psychological tactics

Almost everything is fair in bicycle racing, and psychological tactics are employed regularly. Some racers become very irritated when yelled at, when you persist in drafting, or when you refuse to let them pass. Whatever their weaknesses, take advantage of them. You can sometimes put a competitor out of a race simply by being aggravating. You do nothing really wrong except fray his nerves, and it's all part of the game. Just don't be caught in a psychological trap yourself. Bicycle racers are quite cagey. They try hard to keep you from knowing their true feelings. They may fake either tired or "rarin' to go" attitudes, using whichever they think will work to their advantage in catching you off guard.

The sprint

Final sprints in road races are not as fast as in track races. This is partly because the racers have already ridden many miles and are far from being fresh. The sprint is usually started much earlier or farther from the finish, the speed building up gradually. Half a dozen or so racers generally fight for top place. Each must judge carefully when to make his supreme try. If you want to get power in a hurry, you may at first stand up and pedal hard. After you have increased your rpm's, you can then settle back onto the saddle and keep your wheels spinning.

Watch the man behind you. He may look as though he is having trouble, but he could be the sly one, riding your slipstream and then turning loose when he feels confident he can beat you to the finish.

Pursuit team consists of four racers who take turns in setting pace. (Photo by Schwinn Bicycle Company.)

5
Track races

For both racers and spectators, track races are exciting. The racers can see each other at all times. They know precisely each other's position and can elect their strategy for winning. Similarly, the crowd can see all of the racers simultaneously. They cheer their champions loudly. They boo when a racer makes an objectionable move. Tensions build, and the racers push themselves to the limits of their endurance.

From the late 1800s until the early 1930s, track races were extremely popular in the United States, and there were champions in both World and Olympic events. Then interest in the sport in the United States unexplainably dropped to almost zero. Only since the late 1960s has the interest in bicycle racing begun to climb again. Today more than a dozen tracks or velodromes, all of them outdoors, are in operation in the United States, and a dozen more are in the planning stages. Canada also has about half a dozen bicycle racing tracks. Europe has many more, both indoor and outdoor, for there the sport has never waned.

Tracks

Most of the tracks currently in use in the United States exceed 400 meters (¼ mile). Because of their length, they need relatively small banking. In tracks with a shorter circumference, a banking of 40 to 50 degrees is not uncommon. This permits the racers to lay their bikes far over on the turns without danger of hitting their pedals while they continue to travel at speeds of over 40 miles per hour. Some

Racers ride in a close pack on a banked track, waiting for a chance for a breakaway. (Photo by Keith Kingbay.)

indoor tracks have been no more than 150 meters (less than ⅛ mile) in circumference, and they are steeply banked. The surface needs a smooth texture that is impervious to weather and that will not tear the flesh in case of a fall. Currently the tracks in the United States are surfaced with concrete, macadam, or blacktop, but new surfaces are being developed and tried. The majority of tracks in the world are made of wood, with either teak or cedar preferred. Almost all inter-

national track records have been established on wood tracks, which are especially fast and smooth.

Track racing events of more than a dozen different kinds are staged regularly. Only the most common are described here. In all of these events, of course, a track bicycle is used.

The 1,000-meter time trial

In this event, staged at almost every track race, a single rider is timed from a standing start to the finish line to get an accurate check of his speed. To keep spectators interested and informed, a large and easily read clock may be available, recording the rider's speed while he is underway. The start is very important. If a racer can move from the starting point at nearly top speed, he has a chance to win, but every tenth of a second counts. To get attention these days, however, a racer must cover the 1,000 meters in something less than 1 minute 15 seconds.

For those involved in the race or who have a sophisticated appreciation and understanding of bicycle racing, time trials are exciting. For newcomers to the sport, time trials are not the most interesting introduction to the sport.

Pursuit races

In the individual pursuit race, ranked as one of the most exciting of all bicycle racing events when it is understood, the distance is 4,000 meters (5,000 for professionals, 3,000 for juniors and women). Two racers are started at opposite sides of the track, and to win a racer must either catch his opponent, which rarely happens, or cover the distance in the least time. Speed is obviously the most important factor in this contest, and a superior long-distance rider is most likely to win. Knowing an opponent's riding style is important. He may ride at a fast, steady pace for most of the race and then finish fast, or he may be the kind who burns himself out before the finish.

Team pursuits call for even more precise riding. In these events, there are two teams with four men on each. Each team rides the course in single file, the team members shifting their positions, taking turns setting the pace. It is the clocked time of the third man to cross the finish line that is recorded to determine the winner. To win in a team pursuit race, it is absolutely essential for the members of the team to be matched in their abilities. They should have worked together long enough to function as a single unit.

Match sprint races

Match sprinting, 1,000-meter rides between two competitors, is as much technique and psychology as speed. Since tactics play such an important part, only the last 200-meter segment is timed.

The race is started as an elimination between the entries. Usually, the better riders are put into one category, the others into another. Selection between the two groups relieves the possibility of the two top riders meeting in the first match. In many cases, three or even four riders ride together in the first round. The winners of the heats advance to the ⅛ finals. Usually those who lost in the first round or the ⅛ finals ride again in elimination events known as a repechage. Thus a rider must lose either two or three times to be eliminated.

The race is marked by an explosive finish after usually 500 or more meters of jockeying for position. Often the riders will stand absolutely still, waiting for their opponent to take the lead and be easily watched. Riders may not ride backwards to gain an advantage. In the past, several important matches lasted for more than half an hour, so the allowable maximum time for standing still is now controlled by regulations.

In match-sprint race (above), riders play a cat-and-mouse game, each trying to outmaneuver the other—sometimes standing completely still. (Photo by Schwinn Bicycle Company.)

In tandem sprints (below), the two riders must function as one, each anticipating and responding perfectly to the other's moves. (Photo by Schwinn Bicycle Company.)

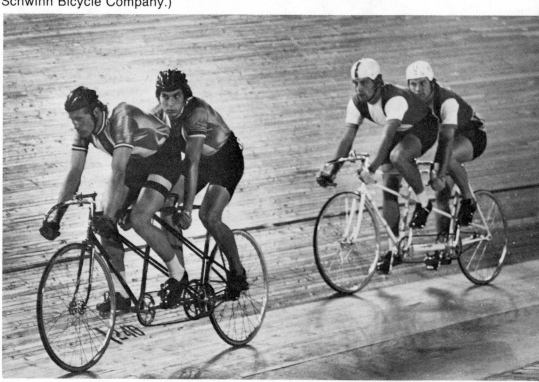

Tandems are also raced in sprints. The distance is 1,000 meters, and the timing to determine the winner starts at the final 200 meters. The speed attained is high—40 miles per hour or more. To operate a tandem successfully in a race, the two riders must function as one, each anticipating the other's changes in pace.

Mass-start races

These races are comparable to the criterium road races but are staged on a track. The typical events are 10 miles or 20 kilometers, but many are more often up to 1 hour or 50 kilometers (31 miles). In points races, the usual distance is 10 or more miles. Sprints for points at prearranged distances decide the winner. Often double points are awarded in the final sprint. In case of tie points, the placing in the final sprint decides the final placing. All kinds of racers have an equal opportunity in the mass-start race—the good pursuiters, final sprinters, or even those who ordinarily ride only in road races. Each rider employs the methods and tactics he has developed for his particular riding skill. Spectators are treated to attacks, breakaways, and almost unbelievably fast sprints.

Often in mass-start races a prime (prize) is given to the leader on each lap. It is indeed possible for a racer to win by this total tally even though he does not come in first in the finish, or win any of the sprints.

In the "unknown distance" race, the riders do not know how many laps constitute the race. When a loud horn or a bell is sounded, they know that the race has only one more lap to go, and the final sprint is a furious one.

Miss-and-out races

These races are similar to mass-start races, but the last racer in each lap is eliminated, until only a few racers remain. These are then given the signal that only one or two laps remain in the race, and they sprint to the finish.

The miss-and-out race is also called the devil-take-the-hindmost, or the elimination race, and it is one of the most exciting of the track racing events for spectators.

Team races

The race itself, a highly interesting one to knowledgeable fans and to the top riders, is usually over a specified time rather than a specified distance—from one or two hours up to the famous six-day races. Teams consist usually of two riders (attempts have been made to have three-man teams) who ride in relay fashion. One rider of the team must be on the track at all times. The relieved member of the team may, as circumstances dictate, either go off the track for a rest or ride slowly around the track until ready for an exchange.

Exchanges are often made at high speed, the relief rider coming lower on the track and then being pushed into the fray by his partner. Today most team riders wear, in a pocket over their left hip, a "jamming tool," which is a roll of tape or cotton to be used as a handle by their partner.

If teams have equal mileage, the race is decided by the points earned by the teams in sprints. If a team is a lap ahead, it wins regardless of the point standing, hence there are fast, exciting jams as teams fight to gain a lap over their competitors. Conversely, a team a lap behind the leaders cannot win regardless of the points gained in the sprints.

While the field is intact (all teams together), they all sprint at the same point. In a long race, a team may be a lap down but gain a considerable number of sprint points and at the last moment rob the early lap leader of victory.

The name "Madison" is taken from Madison Square Garden, which was the location of the early six-day races. At first the racers rode continuously for 147 hours—from 9 P.M. on Sunday until 12 midnight the following Saturday. In

A "change" in a Madison race: the
rider in front pulls his relief rider into
the race by the jamming tool carried
in his partner's hip pocket.

this way they evaded the Sunday "blue laws," the humane societies, and the doctors—all of whom were opposed to the gruel of the six-day event. But it was the riders themselves who evolved the idea of teams to make the races more tolerable.

Six-day races have not made a comeback in the United States because of a variety of factors, but they continue to be popular elsewhere in the world. They have actually been changed to six nights of team races, with cumulative points determining the winners. Novelty events are often added to spark spectator interest and to allow the riders additional rest.

In 1884, the first six-day race was won by Bill Martin, who rode an ordinary (i.e., a "high wheel" bicycle) 1,444 miles in six days. Teams of riders have often exceeded 2,500 miles in the six-day events.

Motor-paced races

Motor-paced races are the fastest of all the track events in bicycle racing. In official events, the bicycles ridden have a small front wheel, necessitating a backward-slanting front fork. The racers are paced by a motorcycle on which the driver stands up to help draft the racer behind him. In this position, too, the motorcycle driver can hear better if the racer, or stayer, shouts to him. In fact, the ear flaps on his helmet are faced to the rear to shield out noises in front and to pick up more clearly those from behind. The driver of the motorcycle and the bicycle rider are considered a team, and the award for winning is given jointly. It is actually the pacer who decides when it is advantageous to attack, when it is best to maintain a particular speed, or any other tactical maneuver. The motorcycle is equipped with a roller bar behind the rear wheel to keep the bicycle at a safe distance behind it.

Motor-paced events are fast, bicyclists maintaining speeds of 45–50 miles per hour. Note the small front wheel and large front sprocket on stayer bicycle. (Photo by Schwinn Bicycle Company.)

In motor-paced races, bicyclists maintain speeds of 45–50 miles per hour. Because the front tire of the bicycle may strike the roller a number of times, it is wrapped to the rim. The gears are large, and the riders are pushed until they have enough speed to keep their vehicles in motion.

Official motor-paced races are now either 50 kilometers (formerly 100 kilometers) or are of one hour's duration. Formerly, larger machines, with the pace-setter positioned more to the rear on his vehicle, made much greater speeds possible; but accidents, including fatalities, forced a change in the rules. In 1927, Leon Van Der Stevft rode over 75 miles in one hour.

Derney-paced races

In derney-paced races, regular track bicycles are used, and the pacing machines are less powerful and are pedal-assisted. These races are not as fast. Often derneys are used to keep up a fast pace in open events.

A racer "sits in" or drafts rider in front of him, riding close to allow him to break the wind. (Photo by William Dunlap.)

6

Track racing techniques and tactics

Tactics are important in successful track racing, even in the one-man time-trial events. In these events, it is often strategy that determines who wins the race—assuming, of course, that he also has the muscles to back up his decisions with instant speed and the reflexes to make his moves count.

Time trials

In time trials, techniques and tactics take a back seat to pure speed and determination; the racer must, however, condition himself to making explosive starts and then to maintaining his speed for the full length of the event, battling a stopwatch and his knowledge of his own time in the past. By compilation of times of the other riders and a study of the track, a racer calculates the time he must achieve to win. A helper, or coach, usually stands alongside the track and signals at predetermined places whether the rider is on or behind schedule. All the racer can do is set his mind to win,

47

and then maintain the swift, smooth pedaling rhythm to make it possible. A steady, unwavering speed with enough power left to cross the finish line is the goal. A racer does not dare let his power die just before the finish line. Tenths, even hundredths of a second, often determine the placing in big events.

Sprints

Sprints, in contrast, call for a maximum of both tactics and speed. If two riders are otherwise equally matched, it is generally the more experienced or the more wily one who wins. He has faced all of the possibilities before and can make those swift decisions that are the difference between winning and losing. Know your opponents. Some are good for a long dash to the finish line. Others like to chase the leader, letting him break the wind and then passing him at the finish line.

In sprints you are on the track with one or more competitors. If you know them, you know whether they are fast at the finish—the final 200 meters—or whether they tend to burn themselves out early and then are tired at the finish. No racer can maintain his fastest speed for much longer than 200 or 300 meters, which is why the timing is done in those final distances. The race is thus actually determined in its final 10 seconds or so.

If you are very fast on a breakaway, it may be to your advantage to draft your competitor. This position will cost you about 15 percent less energy than your competitor, and you will be ready to make your jump over the finish at the appropriate time. Knowing how to draft can help you win, true, but the bottom line always is your muscles against your competitor's muscles to put you in front at the finish.

Once you get the lead, you have to fight to keep your position. If you have not managed to put a large distance between you and the racer just behind you, you must maneuver to keep him on your tail and unable to attack. Lean your bicycle in his direction to make the passing unsafe. Force him toward the rail to scare him into letting up, even slightly, on his pedaling tempo while at the same time you increase your own. It really does not take much to make the difference when the finish line is close, and you must be versatile enough to adapt to the circumstances of the moment. Don't go under the sprinters' line until necessary, but don't allow him room to go under you. In the last 200 meters the leader has the advantage, especially if he has not entered the sprinters' lane.

Pursuit races

Pursuit races call primarily for speed and stamina. The racers are started on opposite sides of the track, but the opportunities for employing tactics are still very real. The racers can tell at a glance whether they are leading or are behind, and based on what they know about their opponent's riding pattern as compared to their own, they can decide whether it is best to take the lead initially and maintain it or to keep about even and then pour it on in the final one or two laps.

In team pursuits, the most important consideration is the ability of the four members to work together as a single unit. They must recognize each other's strengths and weaknesses, then put them to work in ways that assure their winning. The stronger man, for example, may take the lead when the team is riding into the wind and allow the others to draft. If all of the riders on a team are roughly equal in speed and endurance, each may take a turn at front. The changes and dropbacks are done rapidly, every lap or even more often. Whatever technique is elected, the objective is the same: to attain a fast speed and then to maintain it for the duration of the event. If the team wants to increase its speed, all must accelerate together. In teamwork, there is no toleration of the individual. Often one man is sacrificed at the last mo-

A pursuit team rides in echelon—a staggered pattern that protects riders from crosswind.

ment, having worn himself out in a dazzling pace-setting effort. He allows the other three to finish. At this point, the fastest of the finishers is usually the last in line but is ready to overtake his teammates at the line, since it is the third man who is timed.

Mass-start races

Mass-start races combine all of the techniques and tactics, each racer employing the strategy that has worked best for him in his specialty. The good long-distance racers try to get ahead early to establish such a dominating lead that the sprinters, who are tremendously fast but only for short

distances, cannot overtake them with a burst of speed near the finish. But the sprinters will work hard to keep the overall pace slow to make their final sprint most effective. Often several hard pluggers work together, two or more riders exchanging pace during the event and thus working together until the final sprint.

In many important events, racers from the same teams or the same countries commonly work together, one or several riders sacrificing themselves by blocking to turn the race in favor of a preselected man. Sometimes this involves going to the front of the field and then slowing down to allow the selected rider to gain more distance. When points or primes are given for the first racers over the finish line in each lap, a fast racer may decide to get his points early and to let the endurance men battle for the final sprint. As he rides, a racer automatically scores, in his mind, not only his points but also those of the other racers. Good riders, of course, have people in their camp to fight for favorable decisions and to keep them thoroughly informed. They know precisely what it will take to win and spend their energy accordingly. Don't be fooled into chasing every turkey who jumps the field. This takes much of your precious energy.

Similar mental computations can be used in the miss-and-out race, but in this event you are daring elimination if you persist in hanging back, riding the tail of the pack. In this position, you can easily be dropped. But there are some racers who do elect to ride in this position, trusting their ability and the circumstances to be in their favor and permitting them, on each lap, to move far enough ahead to prevent elimination. They save their real power for the final sprint, intending then to move from the rear to the front and over the finish first. This, though, is a wearing tactic, much like being on the end of a crack-the-whip. It is safer and more comforting to be at least in the middle of the field and close to a couple of the best riders.

Team races

Team races consist of two (sometimes three) racers. They change or relay regularly, as they pass on the track or at predetermined times. Some teams work their changes so that the faster of the two is in the race each time there is a sprint for points. In the typical race, for example, there may be 200 laps with 20 sprints or one every 10 laps. In Madisons, perhaps more than in any other track event, it is experience that pays off, a team not only becoming expert in performing together but also knowing when it is best to make their breakaways or when simply to hold their place. And the teams must also be able to make their changes swiftly and smoothly. Part of this can be developed in practice, but the final test comes on the track when it is packed with other riders all moving at full tilt.

When to take the lead

Motor-paced racers generally like to take the lead as early as possible and will fight hard to maintain it. When there are half a dozen or more motorcycle-bicycle combinations on the track, they create in their wake a tremendous current of air. Once caught in this turbulence, a racer can have difficulty pulling out of it even to challenge the lead position. He may even be so buffeted by the wind that he cannot stay behind his own motorcycle.

You may decide, however, that you prefer to start out at the rear of the group until you see how the others are performing and then push yourself forward at what you consider to be the most appropriate time. By the rules of the event, all of the attacks must be made on the right—on the track's banking. If two or more decide to attack at the same time, each traveling at speeds exceeding 45 miles per hour, the experience can be unforgettable.

Vigorous daily training keeps bicycle racers fit for top competition events. (Photo by William Dunlap.)

7
Training

Racers training for top-notch competition maintain a vigorous daily routine, with only occasional short letups. But the rewards are great. The top professionals are among the highest paid and most respected athletes in the world. Long after their competitive careers are over, they are still highly respected, and during their racing careers, they will have traveled over most of the world. But getting to the top is a demanding struggle, with only the most persistent and the fittest surviving.

Some riders are natural sprinters; others are best at long-distance racing. A few are really all-around riders. If you are new at racing, do not make up your mind which kind of racing you want to do. First, try the different kinds and find out which you are best at doing. Your coach or trainer can help you decide what type of racing is best for you and can also help set up the best training program to achieve your goal.

Bicycle racers come in all shapes, sizes, and types. If there were a stereotype, the long-distance road racer would be described as placid in temperament, leggy and lean in physique, with less weight to haul up the hills. The track man, in contrast, would be characterized as a more excitable type, heavier and stockier, with large and powerful thighs and shoulders. These are generalities, of course. Both types require special conditioning to hone their attributes to razor-edge sharpness.

If there is a racing club in your area, join it. It is easier to train and get the needed savvy with a group. The United States Cycling Federation (Box 669, Wall Street Station, New York, New York 10005) can put you in contact with the nearest club.

Training for bicycle racing is much the same as training for any sport that requires aerobic capacity as well as quick muscular coordination. You are probably already somewhat conditioned, but now you will need a steady routine. When you train is not nearly as important as how you train. If your school or work schedule permits, an early training period is best. If not, you will need to hurry home to get in the needed time. A local sport club, sport doctor, or athletic coach can help you start on a systematic schedule. When you are selecting a coach or adviser, make your choice someone you will listen to with trust and respect. Your bicycle is your primary training tool, of course. Put it in fine operating condition and then have it fitted to you.

Form

Look at pictures of good riders in action—not advertising pictures, but photographs of real racers or of racers who are training. Note the position of their feet and arms and also the height of the saddles. This will give you a start or guideline. All of the successful riders will have similar positions or forms, but each is also personalized. You can make those final adjustments after you have been riding for a while and recognize what is needed.

Training on the bicycle

On your bicycle, ride in a fairly low gear (easy pedaling) for the first few miles. The secret of successful bicycle racing is maintaining a steady high-speed pedaling rate. You can never develop this speed by using high gears. As you warm up, pick up your speed. Slow down to a crawl and then burst into top speed for a distance of three telephone poles or so. Then slack off again and repeat the maneuver. Being able to explode into top speed is important when you want to attack or are being attacked in races. Also learn how to charge up the hills, pulling on the handlebars and lifting with the rear foot against the toe clip as you climb.

Keep a diary of your rides and the times. Be honest with yourself. As you progress, your daily rides should become longer—50 or 60 miles. If you are going into longer races, you should go on rides of 100 or 125 miles once or twice a week. Many top riders do 400 to 500 miles per week in their training programs.

Remember to warm down after a hard ride. Ride slowly for a couple of miles, and when you get off your bicycle, swing your arms, twist your body, and flex your fists to get the blood circulating to these areas.

Training off the bicycle

You will need some upper body conditioning to develop your arm, chest, and shoulder muscles. Weight lifting is excellent for this, but avoid the really heavy weights. Smaller weights, and repetitions, are much better.

Do not expect muscles to show up as soon as you start training. Conditioning takes time. You may make rapid gains and then stay on a plateau for a period of time before results can be detected.

For winter training, many bicycle racers use rollers, and some racers also use their rollers for warm-ups before events. Roller races are sometimes staged. The distances are short (usually 2 miles), but the speeds attained are as much as 60 miles per hour. For spectators, speeds are shown on a big dial that records each racer's speed separately. A third arrow records either distance or time.

In most of the United States, there are periods of weather in which training on a bicycle outdoors is not practical. For these periods of cold weather, cross-country skiing is a marvelous exercise for strength and for cardiovascular and aerobic conditioning. Ice skating is another excellent conditioner and will give you the snap and explosive force you need in bicycle racing.

Rollers, the bicycle treadmills, are used by many cyclists to help develop balance as well as high pedaling cadence and skill. Rollers are best ridden with a track bicycle or some other bicycle that has no coasting mechanism. Some riders also use rollers to help them warm up before an event. No athlete should go from a resting position into a contest without first warming up.

An increasing number of riders train on exercise bicycles or on ergometers that have devices for measuring work load and thus give them control over the energy expended. An ergometer enables you to repeat daily your previous performance or to change it as your conditioning dictates. If you do use either of these machines, change the pedals, saddle, and handlebars to match those on your bicycle so that you duplicate as nearly as possible your regular riding position. Measure especially the saddle angle, the distance of the saddle behind the hanger bracket, saddle height and position of the handlebars.

Riding a bicycle generates a tremendous amount of heat that is normally dissipated as the cyclist moves through the air. But on rollers or exercisers, this heat builds up and results in profuse sweating. This can be offset by using a fan that blows over the body, simulating an actual riding situation.

Nutrition

In a strenuous regimen, food is an important consideration, of course. Most coaches, doctors, and athletes suggest a

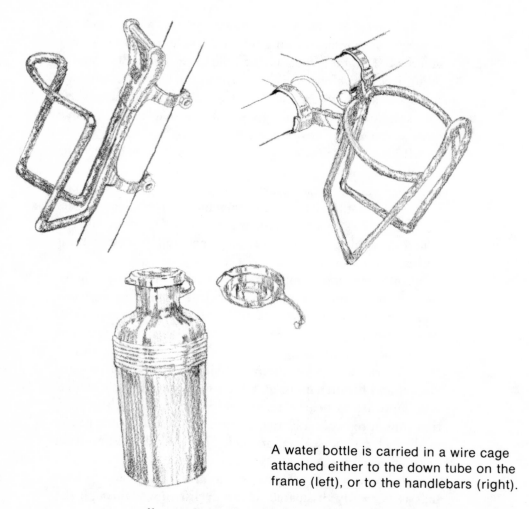

A water bottle is carried in a wire cage attached either to the down tube on the frame (left), or to the handlebars (right).

well-rounded or balanced diet without greasy or fatty foods. Avoid faddish food diets and follow the advice of a competent food nutritionist or your doctor, who can tailor a diet to your specific demands and needs.

Bicycling also requires frequent replacement of body liquids. Keep a water bottle on your bicycle and drink frequently. Taking in about four ounces every 15 minutes is generally recommended, but depending on your system and the riding conditions, you may need a bit more or less. Take drinks before you are thirsty, however, to replace lost fluids before your system begins making demands. Most doctors feel that water is more quickly and easily assimilated by the body than are the synthetic drinks that cause a rush of blood to the stomach and away from the muscles. On long, hard rides, carry along not only water but also some food. Raisins, nuts, bananas, or quartered and peeled oranges—these are examples of the kinds of food that you should take with you.

Bicycle maintenance

Don't forget to keep your bicycle in perfect working condition at all times. Know its quirks and peculiarities as well as its good points, and the primary or routine maintenance is up to you. It is not necessary to take your bicycle apart every week or two. Dismantle the hub or hanger only when it feels gritty. You will know when this should be done. But there are other maintenance checks that you should do routinely.

Check your saddle; it may loosen up. Check the handlebars and handlebar stems. Check your pedals and toe clips. Also examine the brakes, brake handles, chain, derailleur, fork, and sprockets. Problems with these, of course, are generally obvious. Clean and lubricate the chain, derailleur, brake pivots, brake, and derailleur cables. Use a good, light, non-sticky oil. Several times a year grease the cables with a high-quality, nonoxidizing grease. Always keep the derailleurs, brakes, and cones adjusted. Only the hub cones will require a special wrench. Replace worn or frayed cables. Check the sprockets for wear or looseness.

Inspect your tires for cuts or bruises. As you get into racing more seriously, you will undoubtedly have separate wheels and tires for racing. Make certain they are securely glued to the rims if you are using tubulars, which are the regular racing tires. Make these checks yourself. Do not depend on anyone else.

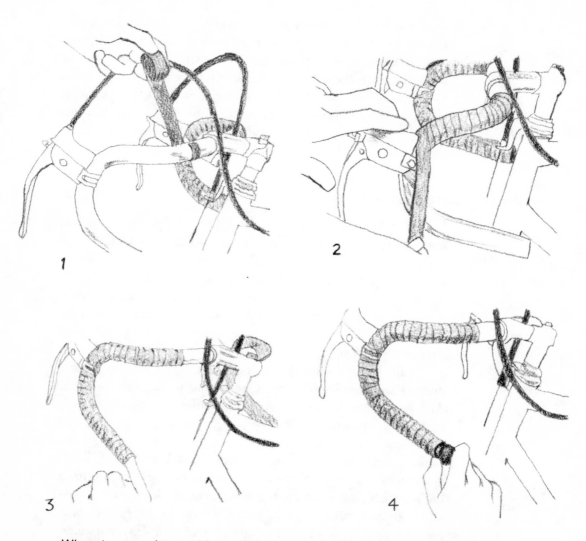

When tape on dropped bars shows wear, replace it with new tape as shown in the steps here. Start the tape about two inches from the handlebar stem and begin winding toward the end of the bar with about ⅛-inch overlap on each wind. Remove brake-lever hoods and wrap tape around the brake-lever brackets in a "figure eight" pattern with ¼-inch overlap. Continue to the end of bar, leaving about ¼-inch overlap of tape that is pushed into the hollow end of bar. Insert end plug to hold in place.

Check the wheels. A broken or loose spoke strains the others in a wheel tremendously. Unless you are very proficient, have a professional true your wheels. This is an art. A wheel out of true (or out of round) uses a great deal more energy, and loss of energy causes loss of speed.

Winning the race depends on how smoothly and efficiently your bicycle operates. Your safety—even your life—is at stake, too.

Enter as many local and regional events as possible. Winning these leads toward state and national championships—and eventually the Olympics. (Photo by Schwinn Bicycle Company.)

8

Bicycle championships

If you enjoy bicycle racing, you may want to progress from local events into the world of championship bicycling. Your first step is to become a licensed rider. In the United States, organized bicycle racing is controlled by the United States Cycling Federation (U. S. C. F.), and you can contact them at the address given on page 56 for the name of your district or state representative. This will give you an opportunity to meet the best competition in your area. It will broaden your knowledge of bicycle racing and open up a world of exciting trips and fascinating memories.

For amateur bicyclists, the ultimate goal is the Olympic Team, but it begins at a grass-roots level. Join a club if there is one near where you live. Through the club you will be kept up to date on when and where races are held in your district of the U. S. C. F. In most clubs, too, you can benefit from the knowledge and experience of people who have been involved with racing over a period of years. From these riders you can learn training methods and racing techniques that will help you attain your goal. They can also help you decide what types of events you should train for, based on how you ride and your physique or temperament. But keep flexible at first. You will discover also that, regardless of your age, there are events that you can enter, and the more competitions you enter, the more confident you become.

State and national championships

First the various state championships are decided. Events contested are for Midget boys and girls (9 through 11), Intermediate boys and girls (12 through 13), Junior boys and girls (14 through 17), Senior men and women (18 and over), and Veteran events (over 40). The winners in the state competitions are eligible to compete for National Championships that are held in a different area of the country each summer. The National Champions are awarded a gold, silver or bronze jeweled medal, depending on their position, and they also get a stars-and-stripes jersey. These colorful jerseys can be worn only by national champions.

International contests

From these National Championship events and sometimes also by separate tests, teams are selected to be representative in the Pan American Games, which are much like the Olympics but with all of the contest senior men from countries of the Western Hemisphere. These games are contested every four years in the year immediately preceding the Olympic Games.

The next in importance are the World Championships, in which the United States has been doing increasingly well in recent years. These events are held annually, with men, women, and junior riders in the competition. The representatives are selected at a pre-race training camp.

In amateur sports, however, the Olympic Games are by far the most important. These are held world-wide every four years in the years that are divisible by four. Many riders spend the full four years between events in training, and special training camps are often set up a year in advance. Again, in bicycling, only senior men's teams compete.

PARTS OF THE BICYCLE
(ROAD RACING)

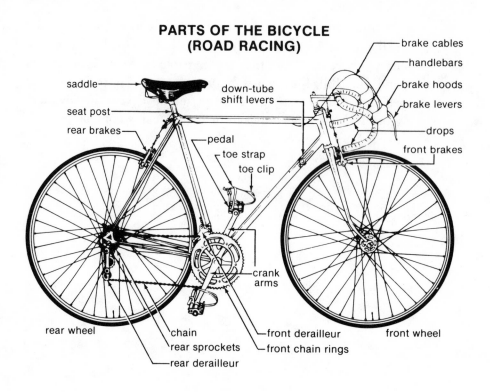

saddle

seat post

rear brakes

down-tube shift levers

pedal

toe strap

toe clip

brake cables

handlebars

brake hoods

brake levers

drops

front brakes

crank arms

rear wheel

chain

rear sprockets

rear derailleur

front derailleur

front chain rings

front wheel

PARTS OF THE FRAME

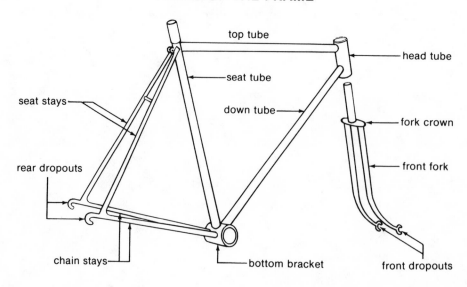

top tube

head tube

seat tube

down tube

fork crown

seat stays

front fork

rear dropouts

chain stays

bottom bracket

front dropouts

Glossary

Ankling—a follow-through pedaling action in which the feet are used in lifting the pedals from the down position as well as for pushing them down; the result is a smooth pedaling movement. At the top of the stroke, the heel is dropped as the ball of the foot pushes forward on the pedal; at the bottom of the stroke, the toe is used to push back on the pedal.

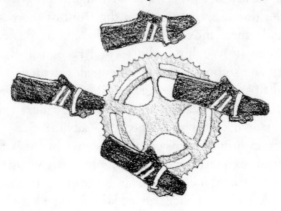

Ankling.

Apron—the flat area below the banked portion of a track; this can be used for other kinds of sports events, such as running.

Attack—the sudden attempt to get away from another racer or group of racers.

Australian pursuit—a pursuit race in which there are three or more riders equally spaced around the track; winner is the racer who passes all his competitors.

Balancing—ability of a racer to sit on his bicycle in perfect balance, motionless and with his feet on the pedals.

Bank—the sloped area of a track; the shorter the track, the steeper its banking.

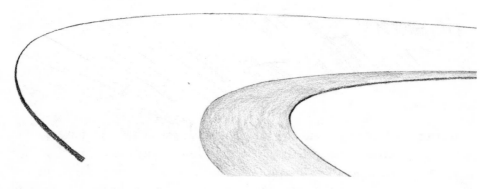

Banking and apron on track.

Bit and bit—a mainly British term describing a riding pattern in which a rider does a short period at the front of the pack breaking the wind, then moves to one side and is passed by the rider immediately behind; the second racer follows the same pattern and so on, each overtaken rider dropping back to the tail end of the pack, then gradually moving forward again.

Blocking—getting in the way to slow down the riders behind, either for your own or for someone else's advantage.

Blow up—to give up in a race, usually because of loss of energy.

Bonk—weak from exhaustion; this results in a **Blow up**, which see.

Bottom bracket—crank mechanism at bottom of frame; a *high* bottom bracket enables racer to pedal full speed through a curve.

Bottom bracket.

Brake—a warning shouted by rider in front for those behind to stop or to slow rapidly because of a hazard ahead.

Break—see **Breakaway**.

Breakaway—a group or groups of riders in front of the main group.

Breakaway.

Bridge the gap—leaving a group of riders and joining another group that is farther ahead.

Bunch—a term for **Pack**, which see.

Burned off—a term for riders who are left behind during a race.

Camp—place with food, drink, and repairs along the road or at a track.

Chainwheel—front sprockets.

Change—in a Madison race, this refers to the relaying of the riders, the one already in the race riding next to his teammate as he is overtaken and either pushing or pulling him into the race; change is sometimes referred to as the **Sling**.

Change.

Chasers—riders who are trying to catch a breakaway group.

Chucker—another name for **Jamming tool**, which see.

Cleats—metal piece on bottom of shoe to hold foot firmly in place on rat-trap pedal.

Cluster—the group of gears or sprockets mounted on the rear wheel.

Cog—rear sprocket or cluster.

Controls—refers to derailleur levers.

Crank—arms to which the pedals are attached.

Crank set—cranks with bearings, cups, and sprockets.

Defend—same as **Blocking**, which see.

Derailleur—mechanism that moves bicycle chain from one sprocket to another to change gear ratios.

Derney—small, pedal-assisted motorcycle for pacing cyclists.

Drafting—taking advantage of another rider's windbreaking by riding close behind him. Taking pace (see **Pace line.**)

Drop-outs—flat metal into which rear wheel on road bicycle is attached.

Echelon—formation in which riders are staggered behind each other for protection from wind.

Field—another term for **Pack**, which see.

Field sprint—sprint of the main group of riders, not necessarily for first place.

Fingertip controls—derailleur levers at ends of handlebars.

Finish line—line across track or road designating the finish.

Force the pace—to ride harder than the other riders, to increase the tempo, or to **Attack**, which see.

Frame size—measurement from center of crank spindle to top of seat tube.

Flange—extension on hub into which spoke is inserted.

Freewheel—rear gear set-up enabling rider to coast when not pedaling.

Hammering—hard pedaling, usually in the big gear.

Handicap race—event in which riders are started off at different times or places so that slow and fast riders are more equally matched. This is the opposite of **Scratch race**, which see.

Handicap Race.

Hand-sling—the changing of partners in a race; same as **Change**, which see.

Hang in—to stay with the group of riders but not taking a turn at front.

Hanger—crank set.

Hanger bracket—part of frame into which crank set fits.

Headset—steering mechanism and bearings on front fork.

Head tube—front vertical tube on frame.

Honk—a term for climbing out of the saddle and standing on the pedals.

Hook—when one rider hits another's front wheel with his own rear wheel, either by mistake or by intent.

Hunger knock—a British term for weakness due to hunger.

Invitational—a special event ridden only by riders who have been pre-selected.

Jump.

Iron—a name for a cheap, heavy bicycle.

Jamming—same as **Hammering**, which see.

Jamming tool—a pad or cloth held securely in racer's special, slim, rear pocket and used as a handle for pulling rider into a race by his teammate in a Madison race.

Jump—sudden burst of speed, racer off the saddle, in a sprint.

Kick—a sudden increase in speed while sprinting at almost the limit.

Leading group—same as **Breakaway**, which see.

Lead-out—an intentional sacrificing tactic in which one rider sprints to give a headstart or advantage to rider on his wheel, who then comes around him at a faster speed.

Madison sling—same as **Change**, which see.

Minute man—in time trials, this is the racer who starts one minute ahead of another.

Musette—bag handed up to rider with food and drink.

Musette bag.

On the drops, hooks, or bottoms—hands on bottom of handlebars.

On the right, left, or below—shouts given by riders in front to warn those behind of obstructions in path as indicated.

On the tops—riding with hands on top part of handlebar.

Open event—a race open to all riders.

Pace line—a single file of riders who take turns riding in front; also referred to as **Echelon**.

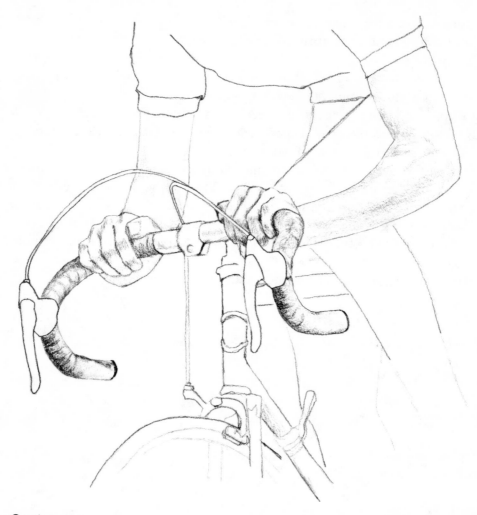

On the tops.

Pack—the main group of riders in a race.

Pedal action—smooth and forceful pedaling, accomplished by **Ankling,** which see.

Peloton—the main group of riders; same as **Pack, Field** or **Bunch,** especially in road racing.

Pole line—line at bottom of track below which riders may not ride.

Position—a rider's form or outline on the bicycle.

Position.

Prime (pronounced *preem*)—a prize within a race for the first to reach a
    certain place or distance.

Pull—to take a turn at the front of the group and then to maintain the
    same speed as before, not trying to get away.

Pull off—to move to the side so that the next rider can take a turn at the
    front.

Pull through—to come to the front and take a turn at leading the pack.

Pursuit—a race against a rider or team starting on opposite sides of the
    track.

Quill—rod inside road axles to tighten wheel into bicycle.

Roller races—events in which rollers are attached to a recording device
    so that riders can compete with their speed and distance
    visible to spectators; generally held indoors.

Scratch race—event in which all of the racers are started together at the
    same time and also go the same distance, as opposed to
    Handicap, which see.

Seat tube—tube extending vertically from hanger bracket into which
    seat post is inserted.

Sew-up—slang for tubular tire.

Sitting in—another term for **Drafting**, which see.

Sitting in.

Sit on a wheel, shelter, be paced—riding close behind another rider and allowing him to break the wind; same as **Drafting**, which see.

Sleigh ride—never taking turn at setting pace; wheel sucking.

Slipstreams—portions of moving air behind a contestant in which it is possible to travel with less effort.

Snap—quick acceleration.

Sprint—a sudden fast burst of speed.

Sprint line—line about 2 feet (70 cm) above pole line.

Stayer bicycle—a special bicycle equipped with a small front wheel and other features; used in official Motorpace races.

String—line of attacking racers forming the front of the pack or field.

Take a flyer—to go off alone in front of the pack.

Time trial—an unpaced race against time.

Top tube—horizontal top tube on frame.

Tubular—racing tire with tube sewn in.

Two-hundred meter mark—line 200 meters (⅛ mile) from finish line.

Warm-up—getting body moving gently to circulate blood before starting vigorous exercise.

Wheelbase—distance between the axles.

Wheel sucking—same as **Sitting in**, which see.

Wind-up—a steady, rapid acceleration; part of a sprint.

Index